# France

Sue Townsend

D0907390

Designed by Tinstar Design
Illustrations by Nicholas Beresford-Davies
Originated by Dot Gradations
Printed by Wing King Tong in Hong Kong


06 05 04 03
10 9 8 7 6 5 4 3 2 1


**Library of Congress Cataloging-in-Publication Data**
Townsend, Sue, 1963-
   France / Sue Townsend.
     p. cm. -- (A world of recipes)
   Includes bibliographical references and index.
   Summary: A collection of recipes from France, plus cultural and
nutritional information.
   ISBN 1-58810-609-8 (HC), 1-4034-3648-7 (Pbk.)
   1. Cookery, French--Juvenile literature. [1. Cookery, French.]    I.
Title. II. Series
  TX719 .T67 2002
  641.5944--dc21

2001004806


**Acknowledgments**
The author and publishers are grateful to the following for permission to reproduce copyright
material: p 5 Corbis; all other photographs Gareth Boden.

Cover photographs reproduced with permission of Gareth Boden.


Every effort has been made to contact copyright holders of any material reproduced in this
book. Any omissions will be rectified in subsequent printings if notice is given to the publisher.

Some words are shown in bold, **like this.** You can find out what they
mean by looking in the glossary.

# Contents

## Key

* easy

** medium

*** difficult

# French Food

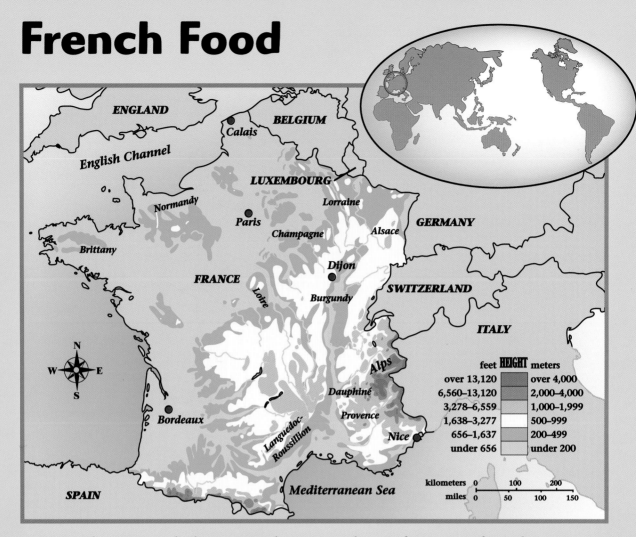

The French love cooking and are famous for their food. The French style of cooking is taught all over the world, and many kitchen tools and cooking terms are known by their French names.

## Around the country

Many types of food are produced in France because it has a varied climate. The north is cooler and has plenty of grass for cows to graze. Milk, butter, cream, and cheese are used in dishes from this area. Many orchards there mean that apple and pear dishes are also popular. Alsace and Lorraine in the northeastern part of the country are known for pastry dishes using local butter and cheeses.

The south has a hotter, drier climate. Here, olive oil is produced and replaces butter and cream in many recipes. In Provence and Languedoc, farmers grow vegetables such as eggplants and tomatoes. In coastal areas, there is plenty of fish to cook.

France is especially famous for its wine. Burgundy, Bordeaux, and the Champagne area produce some of the best-known varieties.

▲ *A wide variety of fruits and vegetables are sold at local markets.*

## Fresh is best

French cooks use a lot of fresh produce. Most towns have a market where shoppers can buy local fruits, vegetables, cheese, fish, and *charcuterie* (pronounced shar-COO-ter-ee). This is the name for cooked and smoked meats and sausages, as well as the name of the shops that sell them.

Every town or village has a bakery. Most French people like to buy fresh bread each day. A long, thin loaf, called a *baguette* (pronounced bag-ET), is especially popular. In France, bread is served with most meals, and people often use it to push their food onto their forks. Pastry shops, called *pâtisseries* (pronounced pa-TEES-er-ee), sell a range of beautiful cakes and pastries.

## French meals

A hot drink, such as coffee or hot chocolate, in a large cup or bowl is common at breakfast with a croissant or bread, butter, and jam. The French enjoy a three- or four-course meal at lunchtime, which might consist of a salad, a meat or fish course, cheese, and dessert. People will eat a lighter meal in the evening.

# Ingredients

olive oil

tomatoes

shallots

zucchini

peppers

onions

salad greens

bread (baguette)

olives

apricots

Camembert cheese

leeks

mushrooms

garlic

chèvre

rosemary

raspberries

Dijon mustard

## Cheese

There are hundreds of French cheeses. Brie, from the northeastern part of the country, is a creamy cheese made in large discs. Camembert, a cheese from Normandy, has a very strong flavor. Both of these cheeses are runny in the center. Other cheeses include *chèvre* (goat cheese), Roquefort, and the well-named Puant de Lille—the stinker of Lille! Specialty cheese shops will have a bigger selection of cheeses than supermarkets.

## Olives

In Provence, in the south, farmers grow olives, both to eat and to make into olive oil. Olive oil is available in all supermarkets. Use the cheaper oils for cooking and the better quality ones for making salad dressings. You can buy whole olives in cans or jars, and sometimes loose from the deli counter of the supermarket.

## Fruit

French farmers grow many different kinds of fruit. These include apricots, currants, strawberries, raspberries, cherries, melons, peaches, apples, and pears. They are all available in supermarkets, but are best when they are in season.

## Vegetables

French cooks use a wide variety of vegetables. More unusual ones include asparagus, artichokes, and wild mushrooms. The French also eat a lot of salad, using many kinds of salad greens. Look for endive, arugula, and chicory in the supermarket.

## Dijon mustard

This mustard is often added to French dishes near the end of the cooking time, or is served alongside meat. It is made of mustard seeds and wine vinegar. Some Dijon mustard is smooth, and some is more grainy. You can buy it in all supermarkets.

## Garlic

Garlic is an important ingredient in French cooking, especially in the south. **Chopped** garlic is available in jars in the supermarket, but the flavor is not as good as that of fresh garlic.

## Shallots

Shallots look like very small onions, but they have a more delicate flavor. They are used to flavor many French dishes. You can find shallots in any supermarket.

# Before You Begin

## Kitchen rules

There are a few basic rules you should always follow when you cook:

- Ask an adult if you can use the kitchen.
- Some cooking processes, especially those involving hot water or oil, can be dangerous. When you see this sign, take extra care or ask an adult to help.
- Wash your hands before you start.
- Wear an apron to protect your clothes. Tie back long hair.
- Be very careful when using sharp knives.
- Never leave pan handles sticking out—it could be dangerous if you bump into them.
- Always wear oven mitts when lifting things in and out of the oven.
- Wash fruits and vegetables before using them.

## How long will it take?

Some of the recipes in this book are quick and easy, and some are more complicated and take longer. The strip across the top of the right-hand page of each recipe tells you how long it will take to cook each dish from start to finish. It also shows how difficult each dish is to make:

* (easy), ** (medium), or *** (difficult).

## Quantities and measurements

You can see how many people each recipe will serve at the top of each right-hand page, too. Most of the recipes in this book make enough to feed two or four people. You can multiply or divide the quantities if you want to cook for more or fewer people.

Ingredients for recipes can be measured in two ways. Imperial measurements use cups and ounces. Metric measurements use grams and milliliters.

In these recipes you will see the following abbreviations:

tbsp = tablespoon       oz = ounce
tsp = teaspoon          lb = pound
ml = milliliter         cm = centimeter
g = gram                mm = millimeter

## Utensils

To cook the recipes in this book, you will need these utensils, as well as kitchen essentials such as spoons, plates, and bowls:

- baking sheets
- food processor or blender
- small frying pan
- large frying pan
- 8-inch round quiche pan
- grater
- heatproof bowl
- measuring cups
- cutting board
- saucepan with lid
- rolling pin
- measuring spoons
- sharp knife
- small screw-topped jar
- shallow, ovenproof dish
- colander
- 4 ramekins or custard cups
- parchment paper
- sieve

 Whenever you see this symbol, be very careful.

# Onion Soup

This soup is often served as a meal in itself in France, especially during winter. Sometimes bacon is cooked until the fat melts. Then the onions are cooked in the fat and the meat is added to the topping.

## What you need

*For the soup:*
3 medium onions
2 tbsp oil
1 tbsp butter
2 vegetable stock cubes

*For the topping:*
3 oz (85 g) Gruyère
    cheese
4 slices French bread

## What you do

**1 Peel** the skin from the onions and cut them in half. Lay each half flat on a cutting board and cut it into thin slices.

**2** Heat the oil and butter in a large saucepan. Add the onions, **cover**, and cook over low heat for eight to ten minutes, stirring occasionally.

**3** Take the lid off the pan and cook the onions until they are a light golden color.

**4** Pour 3 cups (725 ml) of hot water into the pan and bring it to a **boil**. Carefully crumble in the stock cubes and **simmer** for five minutes. Meanwhile, **grate** the cheese.

**5** Put the French bread under the oven broiler and toast one side. Turn the bread over and top with cheese. **Broil** until the cheese has melted and starts to turn brown.

**6** Get a spoonful of soup and blow on it to cool it down. Taste it and add a little salt and pepper if you wish.

**7** Spoon the soup into four bowls and carefully put a piece of the toasted bread into each, cheese side up. Serve, warning diners that the soup and cheese are hot.

# Vichyssoise

This soup, (pronounced vish-ee-SWAZ), is a popular light evening meal in France. This soup can be eaten hot or cold. You may want to add ⅔ cup (150 ml) milk to it if you are serving it cold, to make it less thick.

## What you need

1 tbsp oil
3 leeks
3 medium potatoes
1 chicken or vegetable stock cube
1 ¼ cup (300 ml) light cream (or milk, for a lower fat soup)

## What you do

**1** Trim the tops and roots from the leeks. Cut the leeks in half lengthwise. Rinse them under cold running water to remove any dirt.

**2** **Slice** the leeks thinly.

**3** Heat the oil in a large saucepan. Add the leeks, **cover**, and cook over low heat for five to eight minutes, stirring occasionally.

**4** Meanwhile, **peel** the potatoes and cut them into 1-inch (3-cm) cubes. Take 2 tablespoons of cooked leeks out of the pan and set them aside.

**5** Add the potatoes, 2 cups (475 ml) hot water, and the stock cube to the leeks. Cover and **simmer** over low heat for about fifteen minutes.

**6** Allow to cool for ten minutes. Carefully pour the soup into a blender or food processor (you may have to do this in batches). Put the lid on and process until smooth.

**7** Pour the mixture back into the saucepan. Stir in half the cream and reheat. Take a spoonful of soup, blow on it to cool it, taste it, and add salt and pepper if you wish.

**8** Spoon the soup into four bowls. Pour a little of the remaining cream in a spiral shape on top of each bowl of soup. Place the set-aside leeks on top, and serve.

# Tomato Salad and Green Salad

Fresh vegetables are important items in French cooking. The French would serve either of these simple salads with some crusty bread.

## What you need

*For the salad:*
4 plum tomatoes or
  2 round tomatoes
1 shallot

*For the dressing:*
2 tbsp olive oil
1 tbsp white wine
  vinegar or lemon juice
1 tbsp fresh chives,
  **chopped**
salt and pepper

## Tomato salad

If you can, use plum tomatoes because of their strong tomato flavor.

## What you do

**1** Thinly **slice** the tomatoes and throw away the two end slices. Overlap the slices on two small plates.

**2** **Peel** the shallot, and thinly slice it. Separate the rings and scatter them over the tomatoes.

**3** Put the dressing ingredients into a small screw-topped jar, put the lid on, and shake well. Pour the dressing over the salad an hour before serving if possible, so that the flavors can soak into the tomatoes.

# Green Salad

French markets sell many types of leafy salad greens, all with different flavors. Try using a combination of greens in this salad.

## What you do

**1** Wash the salad leaves in cold water. Pat them dry with a paper towel and put them into a bowl.

**2** Put the dressing ingredients into a small screw-topped jar. Put the lid on, shake well, and pour over the salad. Using a large spoon and fork, gently **toss** the salad to coat all the leaves in dressing. Serve immediately.

## What you need

*For the salad:*
2 cups (75 g) salad greens

*For the dressing:*
3 tbsp olive oil
1 tbsp white wine vinegar or lemon juice
¼ tsp mustard (optional)
salt and pepper

15

# Fish Goujons with Aioli

*Goujons* (pronounced goo-jhon) are finger-length strips of food. In France, cooks use firm, white fish to make *goujons*. If you use frozen fish, **thaw** it overnight in the refrigerator first. Here, the *goujons* are served with a garlic mayonnaise called aioli. If you prefer, add some lemon **zest** or herbs to the mayonnaise instead of the garlic.

## What you need

6 oz (175 g) fish fillets
4 large slices stale
   white bread
1 egg
1 clove of garlic
4 tbsp mayonnaise
3 tbsp vegetable oil
1 lemon
parsley sprigs

## What you do

**1** Cut the fish into strips about the length of your finger.

**2** Cut off the bread crusts. Break the bread into small pieces and use a food processor to make bread crumbs. Pour onto a plate.

**3** **Beat** the egg with a fork in a bowl.

**4** Dip a strip of fish into the egg to coat it. Let any extra egg drip off. Cover the fish with bread crumbs. Lift the strip out and put it onto a plate. Do this with all the *goujons*.

**5** **Peel** and finely **chop** or crush the garlic. Put it into a small bowl and stir in the mayonnaise.

**6** Heat the oil in a large frying pan over medium heat. Add the fish *goujons* and **fry** until golden.

**7** Using a spatula, carefully turn the *goujons* over and cook the other sides.

**8** Cut the lemon into wedges.

**9** Arrange the fish *goujons* on two plates and **garnish** with lemon and parsley. Serve with the aioli.

17

# Quiche Lorraine

This egg and bacon quiche is a specialty of the Lorraine region in northeastern France. If you use a pie crust that is already in a pie pan, **preheat** the oven to 350°F (180°C) and go straight to step 6. You will need a quiche pan with a removable bottom if you use pastry dough that does not come in a pie pan.

## What you need

1 package frozen pastry dough, **thawed** or
1 frozen pie crust

*For the filling:*
4 slices bacon
¾ cup (175 ml) light cream
1 egg
1 egg yolk

## What you do

**1** Preheat the oven to 400°F (200°C).

**2** If using pastry dough and your own pan, roll out the thawed dough until it forms a circle about 12 inches (30 cm) wide.

**3** Carefully lay the dough over the quiche pan, easing it in. Roll the rolling pin over it to trim off any excess pastry.

**4** Prick the dough with a fork and chill for ten minutes.

**5** Lay a 12-inch (30-cm) square of parchment paper onto the dough. Fill it with any type of large, dried beans. **Bake** the dough for ten minutes. The beans will weigh down the dough while it is baking so it stays flat.

**6** Meanwhile, **fry** the bacon until it is cooked. Let it cool, then cut it into small pieces.

**7** To separate the egg yolk from the white, crack the egg open carefully. Pass the yolk between the halves of the eggshell over a bowl until the white has dripped out into the bowl. **Beat** the yolk and the other whole egg together and stir in the cream.

**8** (Omit this step if using a frozen pie crust in a pie pan.) After removing the quiche pan from the oven, remove the beans. Turn the oven down to 350°F (180°C).

**9** Sprinkle the bacon into the crust, pour in the egg mixture, and bake in the oven for about 30 minutes until the filling becomes firm. Serve hot or cold, with salad.

# Pissaladière

*Pissaladière* (pronounced PEE-sa-lah-di-AIR) is a speciality of Provence, in the south of France. It is often served as a starter or light lunch. This recipe uses a food processor to make the base, but you can also use a pre-made pizza crust.

## What you need

2 ¼ cup (300 g) bread flour
1 ¼-oz (7-g) packet active dry yeast
2 tbsp olive oil

*For the topping:*
3 tbsp olive oil
3 large onions
1 tbsp fresh rosemary or thyme
20 to 25 black olives

## What you do

1 To make the dough base, put the flour, yeast, oil, and ¾ cup (175 ml) warm water into a food processor. Process for three minutes.

2 Put the dough into a bowl, cover it with a clean kitchen towel and allow it to rise in a warm place for an hour. Put the dough back into the food processor. Process for two minutes.

3 Sprinkle some flour onto a clean surface and roll the dough into a rectangle about 8 inches (20 cm) by 12 inches (30 cm) long. Place it on a baking sheet, cover it with a clean kitchen towel, and allow it to rise somewhere warm for 40 minutes.

4 Meanwhile, **peel** and **slice** the onions. Heat the oil in a large saucepan and add the onions. **Cover** and cook over low heat for 20 minutes.

5 **Preheat** the oven to 425°F (210°C).

**6** Pull the leaves from the stem of the rosemary or thyme and **chop** them finely.

**7** Add the herb to the onions and cook for two minutes. Spoon the onions over the dough base.

**8** **Bake** on the top rack of the oven for fifteen minutes, then on the middle rack for twelve minutes.

**9** Scatter the olives over the top and serve hot.

21

# Niçoise Salad

Niçoise (pronounced nee-swaz) salad takes its name from Nice, in the south of France. It contains olives and tomatoes, popular ingredients in areas around the Mediterranean Sea.

## What you need

*For the salad:*
4 eggs
⅔ cup (75 g) fresh
    green beans
4 small tomatoes
1 head romaine lettuce
15 to 20 black olives
2 6-oz (170-g) cans tuna

*For the dressing:*
3 tbsp olive oil
1 tbsp white
    wine vinegar
1 tbsp lemon juice
1 tsp mustard (Dijon,
    if possible)
salt and pepper

## What you do

**1** Put the eggs into a small saucepan and cover them with water. Bring the water to a **boil**, then **simmer** the eggs for ten minutes.

**2** Use a spoon to lift the eggs into a bowl of cold water. Keep refilling the cold water until the eggs are cool.

**3** Trim the ends off the green beans. Put the beans into a pan and cover with water. Bring to a boil and cook for three minutes.

**4** **Drain** the beans and put them into cold water.

**5** Cut the tomatoes into quarters. **Peel** the eggshells from the eggs and cut the eggs in half.

**6** Wash the lettuce leaves in cold water and pat them dry with paper towels. Tear them into smaller pieces and arrange them on a large plate.

**7** Scatter the tomatoes, eggs, drained beans, and olives over the lettuce.

**8** Drain the tuna, break it into chunks, and scatter them over the salad.

**9** Put the dressing ingredients into a screw-topped jar and put the lid on. Shake well and pour over the salad just before serving.

# Croque Monsieur

Croque Monsieur, a grilled cheese sandwich with ham inside, is a popular snack in France. If translated into English, its name means "mister crunch."

## What you need

4 slices white bread
4 tbsp butter
2 thick slices smoked ham
3 oz (85 g) Gruyère cheese
2 tbsp olive oil
salad greens to **garnish**

## What you do

**1 Preheat** the oven to its lowest setting.

**2** Using half the butter, spread one side of each slice of bread with it. Place ham onto two of the slices.

**3 Grate** the cheese and put it on top of the ham, leaving a small gap between the cheese and the edge of the bread.

**4** Top each slice of bread with another slice, butter side down. Press firmly all the way around the edges.

**5** Heat half the oil and half of the remaining butter in a frying pan. Put one sandwich in the pan and **fry** on one side over low heat for two minutes.

**6** Carefully turn the sandwich over with a spatula. Fry for two minutes on the second side, until golden brown. Lift the sandwich onto a plate and put it in the oven to keep warm.

**7** Cook the second sandwich the same way, following steps 5 and 6.

**8** Cut both sandwiches in half, garnish with salad greens, and serve hot.

## LOWER FAT VERSION

Because Croque Monsieur is fried, it contains a lot of fat. For a less fatty sandwich, **broil** each side of the sandwich in the oven instead of frying.

# Steak with Herb Butter

Steak served with very thin fries called *frites* (pronounced freet) is a popular meal in France. The fries are sprinkled with salt and the steak is often served with herb butter and a salad.

## What you need

2 small boneless steaks
2 tbsp oil

4 tbsp butter
1 tbsp fresh chervil

2 cups (75 g) mixed
   salad greens

*For the dressing:*
2 tbsp olive oil
1 tbsp lemon juice
½ tsp mustard
salt and pepper

## What you do

**1** Put the butter into a bowl. **Chop** the chervil and mix it into the butter. Place the mixture onto a piece of plastic wrap. Wrap it, shape it into a tube, and put it in the refrigerator to chill.

**2** Place the salad greens in a bowl. Put the dressing ingredients into a screw-topped jar and shake to combine.

**3** Heat the oil in a frying pan until it is very hot. Carefully put the steaks into the pan, then turn the heat down to medium. **Fry** the steaks for four to five minutes on one side.

**4** Using a spatula, turn the steaks over and cook the other side of them for four to five minutes. Place the steaks on two plates.

26

**5** Unwrap the herb butter, cut it in half, and place a piece on each steak. Shake the dressing and pour it over the salad. **Toss** the salad greens with a large spoon and fork to coat them with dressing.

**6** Serve the steak with the salad and French fries or crusty bread.

## HERB BUTTER

Chervil is a leafy green herb that makes tasty herb butter. You can make herb butter with parsley, chives, and other herbs, too. Crushed garlic in butter is also very good.

# Gratin Dauphinois

In the Dauphiné region of southern France, cows graze on the slopes of the Alps mountains. People make cheese from their milk and use it in local dishes such as Gratin Dauphinois (pronounced grah-tan doh-feen-WAH).

## What you need

6 medium potatoes
2 ¼ cup (530 ml) light cream
1 clove garlic
¼ tsp ground nutmeg
3 oz (85 g) Gruyère cheese

## What you do

**1** **Preheat** the oven to 350°F (180°C). **Peel** and thinly **slice** the potatoes.

**(!)** **2** Put the potatoes in a pot of water with a little salt. **Cover** and bring to a **boil**. Remove from the heat and **drain** the potatoes. Put them into a shallow, ovenproof dish.

**3** Pour the cream into a nonstick pan. Peel the garlic, crush it with a fork, and add it to the cream. Add the nutmeg. Gently heat the mixture over very low heat.

**4** Pour the cream mixture over the potatoes. Cover the dish with foil and **bake** for one hour.

**5** Finely **grate** the cheese. Take the foil off and sprinkle the cheese over the potatoes.

**6** Turn the oven up to 400°F (200°C) and bake for fifteen more minutes. Serve hot as a side dish.

## CHOOSING POTATOES

There are more than 200 types of potatoes. Some have a waxy texture when cooked and some have a mealy texture. For this recipe, use mealy pototoes such as russets, because they have the right texture for the dish when they are cooked. Store all types of potatoes in a cool, dark place.

# Mushroom Omelette

In France, omelettes are often filled with ham, cheese, or just a handful of chopped herbs, such as chives or parsley. French people use whatever they have on hand to make omelettes. This omelette uses small mushrooms called button mushrooms.

## What you need

5 button mushrooms
2 tbsp oil
1 tbsp butter
2 eggs
**chopped** herbs
  to **garnish**

## What you do

1 Gently clean the mushrooms and **slice** them. Heat 1 tbsp of the oil in a nonstick frying pan. Add the mushrooms and cook over low heat for four minutes.

2 Add the butter to the pan and heat it gently. Meanwhile, break the eggs into a dish and lightly **beat** them with 2 teaspoons of cold water. Pour the mixture over the mushrooms, covering the base of the pan completely.

3 Cook until the egg starts to become firm around the edges. Using a spatula, push the mixture to the center of the pan. Let the uncooked egg run to the edges of the pan and underneath the cooked egg.

**4** Continue cooking until all of the egg is cooked and firm. Using a spatula, fold the omelette in half and slide it onto a plate. Garnish with chopped herbs.

## VARIATIONS

Try replacing the mushrooms with chopped ham or chopped, cooked vegetables. For a cheese omelette, add **grated** cheese just before folding the omelette in half.

# Ratatouille

In Provence, in the south of France, meals are traditionally left to cook slowly during the day while people work in the fields. This is a quick version of a common dish, *ratatouille* (pronounced rat-a-TOO-ee). It uses many vegetables that grow in the region.

## What you need

1 large or
  2 medium onions
2 tbsp olive oil
2 cloves garlic
1 eggplant
1 zucchini
1 yellow pepper
1 red pepper
1 14.5-oz (425-g) can
  diced tomatoes
1 tsp dried rosemary

## What you do

**1** **Peel** and **slice** the onions. Heat the oil in a large pan, add the onions and **cover.** Cook them over medium heat for about five minutes.

**2** Peel the garlic and crush it into a paste with a fork.

**3** Cut the top and bottom off the eggplant. Cut it into thin slices, and then into cubes.

**4** Cut the ends off the zucchini, and cut it in half lengthwise. Cut each half into 1-inch (3-cm) slices.

**5** Cut both peppers in half and remove the seeds and stalks from them. Slice each pepper half into 1-inch (3-cm) strips, and then into squares.

**6** Add the garlic, chopped vegetables, tomatoes, and rosemary to the onions, cover the pan, and **simmer** over low heat for 20 to 25 minutes.

**7** Spoon the *ratatouille* into a serving dish. Serve with crusty bread, or with meat or fish dishes.

# Apple Tart

## What you need

1 tbsp flour
1 package frozen
  puff pastry
4 apples
2 tbsp lemon juice
6 tbsp apricot jam
powdered sugar
  to **dust**

Apple tarts are popular all over France, but they are a specialty in Normandy, where many apples are grown. If you prefer, use half the quantities listed to make just enough for four servings.

## What you do

**1 Preheat** the oven to 425°F (210°C). Dust a work surface and a rolling pin with a little flour.

**2** Roll the pastry with a rolling pin until it forms a rectangle about 10 inches (25 cm) wide by 20 inches (50 cm) long. Cut the dough in half to make two squares.

**3** Dust two baking sheets with flour and lay the pastry squares on them. **Bake** them for twelve minutes, until they have risen.

**4** Wash the apples and remove their cores. Cut them into very thin slices and arrange the slices in rows on the pastry squares.

**5** Put the lemon juice and apricot jam in a small pan. Heat gently, until the jam has melted, stirring all the time.

**6** Using a pastry brush, coat the apple slices with the lemon juice and jam **glaze**.

**7** Bake the apple tarts for five to eight minutes, until they are golden.

**8** When they are cool, cut each square into four smaller squares.

**9** Put a little powdered sugar into a small sieve and hold it over the apple tarts. Tap the side of the sieve to dust them with sugar.

## VARIATIONS

Try using sliced strawberries, plums, apricots, or pears to make fresh fruit tarts. If you slice it thinly, there is no need to cook the fruit before baking the tarts.

# Crème Brulée

Crème brulée (pronounced crem broo-LAY) is a rich cream **custard** topped with hard caramel. It is especially popular around the Alps, a region famous for its dairy products, but crème brulée is a common dessert all over France.

## What you need

1 ¼ cup (300 ml) heavy cream

1 ¼ cup (300 ml) light cream

4 eggs

3 tbsp sugar

1 tbsp cornstarch

8 tbsp light brown sugar

## What you do

**1** Pour the cream into a medium saucepan. **Beat** the eggs and the sugar together, then stir them into the cream.

**2** Mix the cornstarch with 2 tablespoons of water until it forms a smooth paste. Stir it into the cream.

**3** Gently cook the cream and egg mixture over very low heat, stirring all the time, until it is thick enough to coat the back of a wooden spoon. If the custard begins to form lumps, take the pan off the heat and beat the mixture well. Pass it through a sieve into a bowl, then carefully reheat it in a pan until it thickens.

**4** Pour the custard into four small, heatproof bowls, called ramekins. Leave the custards to cool, then chill them in the refrigerator overnight.

**5** Sprinkle 2 tablespoons of the brown sugar over each custard, making sure the sugar goes to the edges. **Broil** until the sugar has melted and browned.

**6** When the custards have cooled, put them back into the refrigerator to chill competely.

**7** Serve the custards the same day, with fresh fruit on the side if you like.

# Profiteroles

Small cream puffs called profiteroles (pronounced pro-FIT-a-rolls) are used to make a special French cake called a *croquembouche*. A *croquembouche* is a tall pyramid of profiteroles up to three feet high, glued together with caramel.

## What you need

*For the pastry:*
4 tbsp butter
½ cup (60 g) flour
2 eggs

*For the filling:*
1 ¼ cup (300 ml) whipping cream

*For the topping:*
4 oz (115 g) semisweet chocolate

## What you do

**1 Preheat** the oven to 375°F (190°C).

**2** Put ⅔ cup (150 ml) boiling water and the butter into a nonstick saucepan. **Cover** and heat until the butter has melted.

**3** Take the pan off the heat and stir in the flour. **Beat** well with a wooden spoon to make a smooth dough.

**4** Beat the eggs, and then stir a third of them into the dough. Continue adding all of the eggs, a third at a time, beating well.

**5** Scoop up a heaping teaspoon of the dough with a spoon, and push it onto a baking sheet using another spoon. Repeat this to make about 20 balls, leaving an 3-inch (8-cm) gap between each one.

**6** **Bake** the profiteroles for 15 to 20 minutes. Move them onto a wire rack and poke them with a knife to let the steam out.

**7** In a bowl, **whisk** the cream until it becomes firm enough to spread. Chill it for ten minutes in the refrigerator.

**8** Cut each profiterole in half, spoon in some cream, and sandwich the halves together. Pile them onto a plate.

**9** Put the chocolate in a heatproof bowl. Microwave it for one minute, or until it has melted.

**10** **Drizzle** the melted chocolate over the profiteroles from a spoon. Serve right away.

# Tuiles

Formal French meals often end with coffee and a selection of sweets including chocolates and little cookies such as these tuiles (pronounced tweel).

## What you need

6 tbsp butter
2 egg whites
¾ cup (90 g)
    powdered sugar
½ cup (60 g) flour
⅔ cup (100 g)
    chopped hazelnuts
½ tsp vanilla
powdered sugar
    to **dust**

## What you do

**1** **Preheat** the oven to 400°F (200°C).

**2** Melt the butter in a small pan and leave it to cool.

**3** Place sheets of parchment paper onto two cookie sheets.

**4** To separate the egg white from the yolk, crack the egg open carefully. Pass the yolk between the halves of the eggshell over a bowl until the white has dripped out into the bowl. Do this for both eggs.

**5** Put the powdered sugar, egg whites, flour, hazelnuts, and vanilla into a bowl. **Beat** in the melted butter.

**6** Drop teaspoons of the mixture onto the parchment paper, pressing them flat. Leave some space between each one.

**7** **Bake** one tray at a time for eight to ten minutes, until the edges of the cookies begin to brown.

**(!)** **8** Lift the hot cookies off the cookie sheet with a spatula and lay them over a rolling pin so they form a curved shape as they cool. Repeat this for all the cookies as they come out of the oven.

**9** Allow the cookies to cool, dust them with powdered sugar, and serve.

# Chocolate Truffles

Truffles are traditionally served at the end of a special meal in France. The French use the very best quality ingredients to make them, including fresh cream and semisweet chocolate.

## What you need

⅔ cup (150 ml) heavy cream

5 oz (140 g) semisweet chocolate

2 oz (55 g) white chocolate

2 tbsp cocoa

## What you do

1 Pour the cream into a small, nonstick saucepan. Break the chocolate into small pieces and add it to the cream.

2 Heat the mixture slowly, stirring occasionally, until the chocolate has melted. Be careful not to **boil** it.

3 Take the pan off the heat, stir the mixture well and allow it to cool. Chill in the refrigerator for three hours.

4 Finely **grate** the white chocolate onto a plate. Put the cocoa onto another plate.

5 Rinse your hands under very cold water so that the mixture does not melt and stick to them while you are working with it.

6 Scoop out a heaping teaspoonful of the chilled truffle mixture. Quickly roll it between the palms of your hands to form a ball.

7 Place the ball in the grated white chocolate and use a fork to push it around until the truffle is coated in the white chocolate shavings. Set it on a plate.

**8** Repeat step 7 for half the truffles. If your hands are getting sticky and warm, run them under cold water again.

**9** Roll the other half of the truffles in cocoa powder.

**10** Arrange the truffles on a small dish and serve.

## VARIATIONS

In addition to white chocolate and cocoa, you can coat the truffles with finely chopped nuts or coconut, too.

# More Books

## Cookbooks

Denny, Roz. *A Taste of France*. New York: Raintree
Steck-Vaughn, 1994.

Fisher, Teresa. *A Flavor of France*. New York: Raintree
Steck-Vaughn, 1999.

Gioffre, Rosalbe. *The Young Chef's French Cookbook*.
New York: Crabtree Publishing, 2001.

## Books about France

Boast, Clare. *France*. Chicago: Heinemann Library, 1998.

Nickles, Greg. *France the Culture*. New York: Crabtree
Publishing, 2000.

## Comparing Weights and Measures

| | | |
|---|---|---|
| 3 teaspoons=1 tablespoon | 1 tablespoon=½ fluid ounce | 1 teaspoon=5 milliliters |
| 4 tablespoons=¼ cup | 1 cup=8 fluid ounces | 1 tablespoon=15 milliliters |
| 5 ⅓ tablespoons= ⅓ cup | 1 cup=½ pint | 1 cup=240 milliliters |
| 8 tablespoons=½ cup | 2 cups=1 pint | 1 quart=1 liter |
| 10 ⅔ tablespoons=⅔ cup | 4 cups=1 quart | 1 ounce=28 grams |
| 12 tablespoons=¾ cup | 2 pints=1 quart | 1 pound=454 grams |
| 16 tablespoons=1 cup | 4 quarts=1 gallon | |

# Healthy Eating

This diagram shows which foods you should eat to stay healthy. You should eat 6 to 11 servings a day of foods from the bottom of the pyramid. Eat 2 to 4 servings of fruits and 3 to 5 servings of vegetables a day. You should also eat 2 to 3 servings from the milk group and 2 to 3 servings from the meat group. Do not eat too many foods from the top of the pyramid.

The French love fresh fruit and vegetables, as many of the recipes in this book show. For special meals, however, some recipes do use a lot of butter, cream, and cheese. It is healthier not to eat these dishes too often.

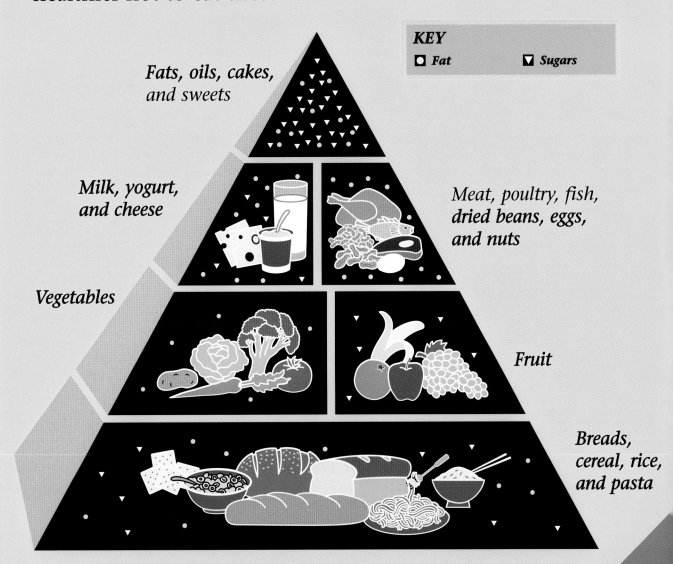

**Fats, oils, cakes, and sweets**

**KEY**
⬜ *Fat*　　▼ *Sugars*

**Milk, yogurt, and cheese**

**Meat, poultry, fish, dried beans, eggs, and nuts**

**Vegetables**

**Fruit**

**Breads, cereal, rice, and pasta**

# Glossary

**bake**  to cook something in the oven

**beat**  to mix something together strongly using a fork, spoon, or whisk

**boil**  to heat a liquid on the stove until it bubbles and steams strongly

**broil**  to cook something under or over direct heat

**chop**  to cut something into pieces with a knife

**cover**  to put a lid on a pan or foil over a dish

**custard**  milk or cream that has been cooked together with egg

**drain**  to remove liquid from a pan or can of food

**drizzle**  to pour something slowly and evenly

**dust**  to sprinkle something, such as powdered sugar, lightly over food

**fry**  to cook something in oil or butter in a pan

**garnish**  to decorate food for serving, for example, with fresh herbs or lemon wedges

**glaze**  to coat the outside of food with a liquid; what the liquid used for glazing is called

**grate**  to shred something by rubbing it back and forth over a utensil that has a rough surface

**mash**  to crush a food, such as potatoes or beans, until it is soft and smooth

**peel** to remove the outside of a fruit, vegetable, or hard-boiled egg

**preheat** to turn on the oven in advance, so that it is hot when you are ready to use it

**simmer** to cook a liquid gently on the stove at just under a boil

**slice** to cut something into thin, flat pieces

**thaw** to bring something that has been frozen to room temperature

**toss** to gently turn over the leaves in a salad to coat them with dressing

**whisk** to beat air into ingredients by beating quickly with a utensil; the name of the wire utensil that is used for whisking together ingredients

**zest** outer layer of peel on a citrus fruit such as an orange or a lemon

# Index